GOD MAKES US DIFFERENT

Written and illustrated by
Helen Caswell

Abingdon Press
Nashville

GOD MAKES US DIFFERENT

Library of Congress Cataloging-in-Publication Data

Caswell, Helen Rayburn.
  God makes us different.
    I. Creation—Juvenile literature.   2. Provi-
dence and government of God—Juvenile litera-
ture.   3. Identification (Religion)—Juvenile liter-
ature.   I. Title.
BT695.C37   1988   241   87-33466

ISBN 0-687-06706-5 (pbk. : alk. paper)

96 97 98 99 00 01 02 03 04 — 10 9 8 7 6 5 4

PRINTED IN HONG KONG

There isn't anybody just like me,
because God makes everybody different.

I guess when God has to make so many people,
it's more fun to make them different.

It would be boring to make them all the same.
So he makes us different colours—
brown and pink and tan.

And he makes all shapes and sizes.

And he puts curly hair on some and straight hair on others.

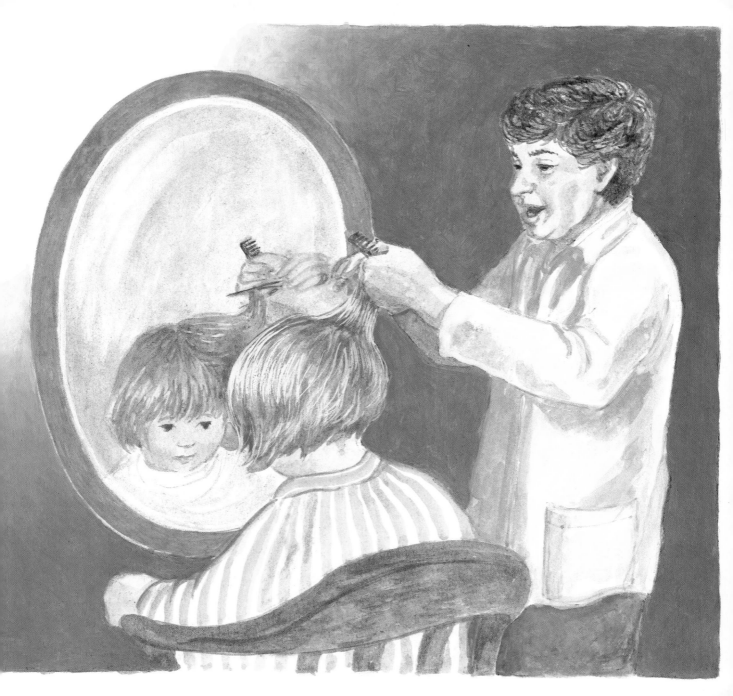

And some are boys and some are girls.

God makes some noisy ones and some quiet ones.

But though people look different on the outside, on the inside, we are not different at all.

Everybody likes to eat.

And everybody needs to sleep.

Everybody cries, sometimes.

And everybody likes to laugh.

So I guess God makes our outsides all different, just for fun.
But he makes our insides all alike,
   and he loves us, every one.